Simple Solutions™

Chewing

Plus Training Tips

By Kim Campbell Thornton
Illustrations by Buck Jones

BOWTIE™ PRESS

IRVINE, CALIFORNIA

Nick Clemente, Special Consultant
Amy Fox, Editor
Michael Vincent Capozzi, Designer

The dogs in this book are referred to as *he* and *she* in alternating chapters.

Library of Congress Cataloging-in-Publication Data

Thornton, Kim Campbell.
  Chewing / by Kim Campbell Thornton ; illustrations by Buck Jones.
    p. cm. -- (Simple solutions)
  ISBN 1-889540-82-X (pbk. : alk. paper)
  1. Dogs--Behavior. 2. Dogs--Training. 3. Mastication. I. Jones,
Buck. II. Dog fancy (San Juan Capistrano, Calif.) III. Title. IV.
Series.
  SF433 .T525 2001
  636.7'0887--dc21
                            2001004822

BowTie™ Press
A DIVISION OF BOWTIE, INC.
3 Burroughs
Irvine, California 92618
949-855-8822

Printed and Bound in Singapore
10 9 8 7 6 5 4 3 2

Contents

Why Do Dogs Chew?

They gnaw on knickknacks, suck on socks, chew on chair legs. Their destructive power is roughly equivalent to that of a minor atomic weapon—at least, that's the way it looks when you discover it. Stuffing pulled out of sofas, new designs nibbled into wallpaper, drywall exposed, wood floors destroyed. All this, while brand-new chew toys lie in the rubble, still pristine.

What causes dogs to chew and chew and chew? And how can you channel their chewing constructively?

Dogs chew for many reasons. Young dogs have a physio-

logical need to chew. Chewing helps them to exercise and develop their jaws. Six-week-old puppies have a set of baby teeth (your veterinarian may refer to them as deciduous teeth). Through the process of teething, all the baby teeth will eventually be replaced by permanent teeth. Puppies start to lose their baby teeth when they're six to seven months old, but permanent teeth don't fully come in until dogs are about one year old. During this time, puppies chew a lot. Chewing helps relieve the pain of teething and is a perfectly normal part of puppy growth and development. One solution to help relieve teething

pain is to freeze an old wet washcloth and give it to your
pup to chew on.

Puppies also go through an intense play period, and

one of the things that puppies do in play is chew. It's fun to chew things up and see the pieces go flying!

Older dogs chew because it's pleasurable or soothing for them. Chewing helps relieve boredom. It also helps keep dogs' teeth and gums strong and healthy. Dogs with irritated or painful gums from gingivitis may chew excessively to help relieve the pain. Some dogs chew when they're feeling nervous or stressed. Often, their chewing results from separation anxiety. In all these instances, chewing is a repetitive activity that's soothing and just plain feels good. Sort of like playing solitaire.

Of all the reasons dogs chew, spite isn't one of them. You may feel as if Max has destroyed your favorite pair of $200 sandals because you don't spend enough time with him, but face it, dogs just aren't wired that way. While they're pretty darn smart, they aren't capable of thinking, *I'll teach her to leave me alone for twelve hours straight. I'll go find her favorite, most expensive pair of shoes and eat them!* The belief that dogs do things to get back at us is a myth that should have been retired long ago.

Now that you know why dogs chew, it's time to examine your dog's chewing habits and your responses to them. Believe it or not, your dog can learn to chew just his toys, not yours. Teaching your dog what's okay to chew and what's not takes patience and consistency, but the savings in money and frustration are well worth the effort. And when your puppy is chewing on a toy, he's not barking, digging, or otherwise getting into trouble.

When Chewing Becomes a Problem

We often think that puppy chewing is cute. We might say, "Look at her toss her head with that envelope in her mouth!" We ignore this cute behavior until something valuable is destroyed, then we want to put a stop to it. By that time, however, the chewing of anything and everything is a habit that's difficult to break.

Preventing inappropriate chewing is not just good for your furniture and clothing but can save your dog's life.

Dogs who chew electrical cords run the risk of death by electrocution. Dogs who steal garbage, cat food, or rich treats are at risk for pancreatitis, a potentially fatal inflammation of the pancreas. Dogs who eat socks, rocks, or

children's toys can suffer life-threatening intestinal blockages.

Destructive chewing is also harmful to your dog, as it frequently causes feelings of boredom, loneliness, and isolation. Dogs are intelligent, social animals who need the stimulation of activity and companionship. The psycho-

logical stress of being left alone on a regular basis can lead to phobias or anxieties that result in chewing as escape behavior (for instance, chewing through doors or windows) or chewing for relief (for example, when the dog is left alone or when a change occurs in the house-

hold, such as a new baby or a new work schedule). Because chewing is so enjoyable and calming, dogs want to do it again and again. That desire to chew can become a good habit or a bad habit, depending on what dogs learn to chew and the quality of interaction they have with their owners.

If you have a puppy, you'll need to start teaching her good habits in puppyhood. Given the opportunity, she's going to chew everything she can get her teeth on. Besides being entertaining, it's simply her way of exploring her territory. When your puppy decides to chew on an electrical cord, it's because she doesn't yet know that the cord isn't a toy like her hard rubber ball or bone. Teaching your puppy right chewing from wrong chewing requires a two-pronged approach: making your home safe for the puppy (and from the puppy) and redirecting improper chewing.

Dog-Proofing Your Home

Just like infants, puppies put anything and everything in their mouths. One veterinarian says he is astounded by the variety of things puppies will chew on or swallow. With that in mind, it's a priority for new puppy owners or owners of chewers to take steps to remove temptations or make them unappealing or inaccessible. (The bonus to this is usually a neater, less-cluttered home.)

Smell is often what first attracts a dog to a forbidden item. Things that smell good to a dog range from stinky socks to leather shoes to ripe garbage. Make it a habit to

put laundry in hampers, shoes in closed closets, and trash containers inside cabinets. If there's no room for the trash beneath the kitchen or bathroom sink, buy containers with locking lids. Avoid small decorative trash cans, which are just the right size for an inquisitive puppy to stick his nose into and pull out such shreddable treasures as envelopes and used tissues. Put small trash cans on top of your dresser or bathroom counter.

Secure heavy items that could fall on your puppy. Remind family members to pick up toys, clothes, remote controls, eyeglasses, and briefcases. Take up throw rugs, and put plants out of reach. Don't leave the ends of toilet paper hanging down. Everything is fodder for the puppy chewing machine.

Dog-proofing your home is more than just keeping things picked up. You need to look at things from a dog's eye view. In each room, get down on your hands and knees so you can see what your pup sees. Doesn't the carving on that table leg look interesting? And look at all those cords underneath the desk where the kids do their homework.

Tape down cords for lamps and electronic equipment. Wrap the cords and bind them with plastic cable ties, (available at electronics stores), or coat them with Bitter Apple or another unappetizing substance, such as hot sauce or a solution of cayenne pepper mixed with water. You can also try covering cords in aluminum foil. Many dogs don't enjoy biting down on the silvery wrap. Avoid wrapping frayed cords with aluminum foil, as it could serve as a conductor for electricity. If cords are frayed, it's best to replace them anyway. They aren't safe, even without a puppy around.

If your puppy shows interest in chewing on walls or furniture legs, coat the attractive area with a nasty-tasting substance, such as Bitter Apple, citronella oil, or hot sauce. (Apply it first in an inconspicuous area to make sure it doesn't harm the finish.) Not every dog finds these concoctions unpleasant; some even seem to think they just add to the flavor. They're worth a try, however.

Forget the idea of giving your puppy old socks or shoes to chew on. He can't tell the difference between those and your good shoes and socks, so don't run the risk of confusing him.

If there's a room in your home that's not safe for a curious dog, keep it off limits with a baby gate or other barrier. Be sure the pup can't stick his head through the gate and get stuck. If baby gates don't work for your situation, close doors or keep the puppy leashed at your side.

Find one room in your home that can be a place where your puppy can go freely. This is usually a kitchen, laundry room, or bath-room. Be sure to stock this room with several approved toys. Even in a "safe" room, however, your pup may take it into his head to nibble on the baseboards, cabinets, or wall. For repairs, keep cans of paint and spackling handy but out of reach.

The most important step in avoiding chewing disasters is, well, preventing them. When you can't be around to supervise, confine your dog to the safe room or to a crate, along with a toy to keep him occupied. That way, he can't get into trouble, and you won't get mad at him.

When a crate is introduced and used correctly, it's a kind, effective way to keep a puppy or dog out of harm's way. Help the puppy feel at home in his crate by feeding him in it, and never use crate time as a means of punishment. If you take these steps, your dog will feel safe in his cozy den—which should be just large enough for him to lie down, stand up, and turn around in—and your belongings will be protected from the depredations of sharp puppy teeth.

If your dog is younger than six months old, don't confine him to a crate or safe room for more than four hours at a

time without giving him an opportunity to take a potty break. Dogs this young simply aren't capable of "holding it" for much longer than that.

What Should Dogs Chew?

Your dog needs a variety of chew toys. She should have at least half a dozen—many trainers recommend more—of different sizes, shapes, and textures. Which toy your dog prefers may depend on her mood or what game she wants to play.

Rotate toys weekly so that only a few are out at any one time. This helps prevent boredom. When you bring out the other toys, they'll seem like new. Place the current week's toys in a toy box or other container your dog can easily access so she can choose what she wants to play with.

Toys for dogs range from the classic rawhides and hard rubber bones to stuffed cuddle toys to interactive items, such as Action Balls or Buster Cubes, which can be filled with bite-sized treats. Whatever you choose should be both practical and long lasting, able to withstand a lot of high-energy play. The best chew toys are safe, fun, easy to clean, inedible, and hard-wearing items that are different from your own belongings.

Avoid toys that resemble or are made from household items you wouldn't want destroyed. This includes toy shoes or tugs made from old socks. It's less expensive to

buy dog toys than it is to replace good clothes or shoes that are mistaken for toys. If your child has a favorite teddy bear or other stuffed animal, be sure it's kept separate from the dog's stuffed animals.

Beware of other toys that contain small hard parts or

bells, buttons, and squeakers that could be swallowed. Rawhide bones are controversial because many dogs gobble them down and can choke or suffer digestive blockages when large pieces are swallowed. Most trainers recommend giving rawhide only under supervision and removing the bone when the dog is left alone. If you choose to give rawhide, look for compressed rawhide, which is less likely to break down in the intestinal tract.

Favorite dog toys are Kongs, Nylabones, Buster Cubes, tennis balls, rope toys, Cressite or other solid-rubber balls, Star Balls, Mutt Pucks, and soft objects, such as stuffed animals or fleece toys, especially those that make squeaky sounds.

Kongs and Star Balls bounce erratically, so they're interesting for dogs to chase. Tennis balls are beloved by

retrievers everywhere. The fibers of rope and sheepskin toys help keep a dog's teeth clean, similar to what flossing does for humans. Handle soft toys frequently so they hold your scent. Your dog will love snuggling with them when you're not home. This is especially important for dogs with separation anxiety.

Buster Cubes, Goodie Grippers, Kongs, and similar toys are great for keeping dogs occupied for long periods because they can be stuffed with treats, such as peanut butter, soft cheese spreads, raw baby carrots, kibble, and biscuits, so that dogs have to work to get them out. Make rubber toys, such as Nylabones or Mutt Pucks, more appealing by coating them with bacon grease, peanut butter, or cheese. (Remember to clean and disinfect all these toys on a regular basis. Most can be run through the dishwasher.)

Special chew treats can be made by stuffing a hollowed, sterilized beef marrow bone with a thick filling of kibble mixed with water. Mix equal amounts of kibble and water and let the mixture sit for an hour to soften. Fill the bone and freeze it overnight, then "frost" the ends with a soft cheese or peanut butter. This is likely to make a mess

as it's chewed, so give it outdoors and under supervision to make sure your dog doesn't swallow any bone fragments.

Even the best toys have a finite life span. Replace toys with broken or sharp edges, loose squeakers, or small, easily swallowed parts. Get rid of rawhide toys that have softened or come apart, as well as rope toys that don't have knotted ends. Sew up or discard soft toys that are coming unstuffed. If your dog has a special favorite, keep a couple of extras of that type of toy so that a replacement is available when the old one bites the dust.

Teaching Your Dog to Chew Toys

Too often we assume that a dog instinctively knows that his toys are there for him to chew, and he may play with them for a time. But he needs to be taught that he is permitted to chew only those toys and not any other household items. This is easy to do using positive reinforcement.

Any time you see your dog chewing on his dog toy, tell him what a good dog he is. To further reinforce his good behavior, try clicker training. Get a clicker at a pet supply store or toy store. When you notice him chewing on his toy, click once, then immediately give him a treat and praise him by saying, "Good chew toy!"

Play games such as fetch with your puppy's toys so he

associates them with good times. Keep toys in every room so your dog always has something good to chew on. Remember to handle toys frequently so they have your scent. You can make them more appealing by stuffing them with treats or peanut butter.

Give each toy a name, such as "red ball" or "rope bone." Dogs can understand large vocabularies, and many are capable of distinguishing between, say, their green frog and their red ball, their bone and their Kong.

When your dog brings you a toy, praise him. Then start putting a name to the action: "Good get your toy!" Start telling him, "Get your toy!" and reward him when he complies. Click, treat, and praise if you're using clicker training.

Another fun game is to scatter toys throughout the house. Walk to each room with your dog, and say, "Find the toy!" When he picks up the toy, reward him with praise and a treat, or click and a treat.

Teach your dog to greet you with a toy in his mouth. When you come home, say, "Find your toy!" or "Get a toy!" Withhold petting or other attention until he's clutching a toy. When he knows it's about time for you to get home, he'll start looking for a toy to chew on in preparation for your arrival.

To test your dog's knowledge of what he should and

shouldn't chew, set out several chew toys, plus a forbidden item, such as a paperback book or a plastic yogurt container. Have a noisemaker handy, such as an empty soda can with a few pennies inside. (Tape the lid so the coins don't fall out.) Say, "Get your toy!" and reward him with praise and a treat if he chooses an appropriate item.

If he picks up something other than a toy, clap your hands, then say, "Aaaack, drop it!" or otherwise startle him into letting go of the item. It may be useful to have a helper who can toss the shake can in the pup's direction (don't hit him with it!) if he picks up the wrong thing. Then

repeat the command to get a toy, and reward him when he chooses correctly. With practice, you should eventually be able to present him with many inappropriate items and only one toy and have him always choose the toy.

Some puppies run away with the item they're chewing. Don't give chase. Instead, run in the opposite direction, encouraging your dog to chase you. If he drops the item when he runs after you, that's good. Give him a toy and praise him. If he doesn't drop it, calmly take the item away when he gets to you and replace it with a toy.

Any kind of positive reinforcement works much better

than punishment when it comes to teaching puppies right from wrong. But there will always be instances when your puppy or dog backslides or tries to chew on something dangerous. In the following section you can learn several ways you can change your dog's behavior and set his jaws back on the right path.

Ways to Redirect Problem Chewing

If you catch your dog chewing on something forbidden, distract her by tossing a shake can or other noisemaker in her direction. The sound should startle the puppy into dropping or leaving the unacceptable item. Then give her a toy, and click, treat, and praise when she chews on or plays with the toy.

Correction is especially important when your pup is trying to chew something dangerous, such as an electrical

cord. You can't afford to let her learn a shocking lesson on her own, so you need to correct the behavior instantly, making it so unpleasant that the dog won't even want to try chewing cords again.

To put a stop to this type of inappropriate chewing, give

the dog an immediate verbal warning that what she's doing is wrong. Call out, "Aaaack!" or "No!" Within two to five seconds—the sooner the better—follow the verbal warning with a physical correction, such as squirting the dog with water from a spray bottle or tossing a throw pillow in her direction (don't hit her with it). Once she's distracted from bad chewing, give her a toy or tell her to go get a toy, then praise her for chewing the toy. Then try to find a way to make the dangerous item inaccessible or unpleasant.

For dogs who are trash hounds, try booby-trapping the

garbage. Place pot lids or empty aluminum cans on top of the garbage can. When your dog tries to get into the trash, the lids or cans will clatter down, startling her with their noise.

If you come home and find something chewed up, there's no point in yelling at your dog about it. She won't understand what she did wrong. Correct her only when you catch her in the act of chewing the wrong thing. Just as important, if not more so, praise her when you catch her chewing the right thing. Remember, as well, that too much punishment and not enough training and praise will simply teach your dog to do her destructive chewing in secret.

You can also prevent destructive chewing by confining the dog when you can't be there to supervise. Crating her or putting her in a dog-proofed room protects your belongings and protects your dog from a scolding that she won't understand. Be sure you give her a safe chew toy that is stuffed with goodies, so she'll have something to occupy her while you're gone. This is especially important for dogs younger than two years of age. Even though they look full grown, they're still puppies emotionally and physically and should not be given free run of the house until they've proven themselves trustworthy.

One of the best ways to avert destructive chewing is to give your dog plenty of exercise. To paraphrase an old saying, idle paws are the devil's workshop. Just like children, dogs need a lot of play to keep them physically and mentally fit. Highly active dogs, such as Labrador retrievers or Jack Russell terriers, need as much as one to two hours of exercise daily. When they don't get enough activity, they turn their clever canine minds to finding their own entertainment, and their choice of entertainment frequently involves chewing.

Take your dog for a half-hour walk in the morning before you leave for work. The exercise will help her relax, making her less likely to chew destructively. Include some

training practice, such as sit-
ting or heeling, while you
walk to give her some mental
stimulation. On a rainy day or
when you're running
short of time, play
fetch in the house
for fifteen or twenty minutes. Toss
a ball down the hall or stairs for your dog to retrieve.
Another walk or play session in the evening will help your
dog settle down for bedtime.

If your dog is chewing excessively or destructively and hasn't responded to training and redirection, take him to the veterinarian to rule out an underlying medical cause, such as a nutritional deficiency. Your veterinarian can also help you figure out if the chewing is related to a phobia or to separation anxiety, or the doctor may refer you to a behaviorist who can help.

Preventing a Chewing Problem

If you have a puppy, spend the time now to keep his need to chew from becoming a chewing problem. To help prevent separation anxiety and related chewing, gradually introduce your dog to the concept of being left alone. Start by leaving him for only five or ten minutes at a time. You need to teach your dog that you will always come back.

Slowly increase the amount of time you're gone, and be sure your dog has toys to keep him occupied. If he has a

couple of favorite toys, consider making them even more

special by giving them to him only at times when you'll be

gone. It can also help to leave the radio or television on so he'll have the comfort of human voices.

When you leave the house, do it matter-of-factly, and when you return, ignore the dog for the first few minutes after arrival. Making a big production out of leaving or arriving gives the dog the idea that being alone is bad and your return is exciting. Instead, you want him to view arrivals and departures as routine. Fun things, such as going for a walk or being fed, should be postponed until you've been home for a little while.

It's also important to teach your dog early on that he

can't get attention any time he wants it. If you are busy and your dog is bugging you for attention, it's okay to put him in his crate for a nap while you complete your task. Instead of petting him or playing with him every time he asks, first require him to perform a command, such as *sit* or *down*. This technique is called "learn to earn" and establishes your leadership.

If your dog is younger than two years of age, consider crating him or leaving him in a safe room or a dog run whenever you can't be there to supervise. Dogs this young are rarely capable of being reliable in the house. It's your responsibility to keep them from getting into trouble. A dog who always receives a scolding when his owner returns home will simply become more and more anxious every time he's left alone. A dog who's confined, however, is unable to get into trouble and, thus, is less prone to anxiety.

Whatever the cause, chewing is not a behavior that your dog will magically outgrow. He needs your guidance to learn what to chew, and spending time with you is the only way he can learn your rules.

Kim Campbell Thornton is an award-winning writer and editor. During her tenure as editor of *Dog Fancy*, the magazine won three Dog Writers Association of America Maxwell Awards for best all-breed magazine.

Since beginning a new career in 1996 as a freelance writer, she has written or contributed to more than a dozen books about dogs and cats. Her book *Why Do Cats Do That?* was named best behavior book in 1997 by the Cat Writers Association. The companion book *Why Do Dogs Do That?* was nominated for an award by the Dog Writers Association of America. Kim serves on the DWAA Board of Governors and on the board of the Dog Writers Educational Trust. She is also president of the Cat Writers' Association and belongs to the National Writers Union.

Buck Jones's humorous illustrations have appeared in numerous magazines (including *Dog Fancy* and *Cat Fancy*) and books. He is the illustrator for the best-selling books *Kittens! Why Do They Do What They Do?* and *Puppies! Why Do They Do What They Do?*

For more authoritative and fun facts about dogs, including health-care advice, grooming tips, training advice, and insights into the special joys and solutions for unique problems of dog ownership, check out the latest copy of *Dog Fancy* magazine or visit the Web site at www.dogfancy.com.

BowTie Press is a division of BowTie, Inc., which is the world's largest publisher of pet magazines. For more books on dogs, look for *Barking*, *Dogs Are Better Than Cats*, *Dogs Rule*, *The Splendid Little Book of All Things Dog*, *Why Do Dogs Do That?* and *Puppies! Why Do They Do What They Do?* You can find all these books and more at www.bowtiepress.com.